Original title:
Laughing Through the Meaning of Life

Copyright © 2025 Creative Arts Management OÜ
All rights reserved.

Author: Oliver Bennett
ISBN HARDBACK: 978-1-80566-011-8
ISBN PAPERBACK: 978-1-80566-306-5

Grins Beneath the Stars

In the quiet of night, we chuckle and play,
As the moon winks back, in its silvery way.
Stars giggle in twinkles, a comet just might,
Make us laugh louder, beneath the starlight.

Thoughts swirl like candy, light and carefree,
Jokes float on the breeze, like leaves from a tree.
With smiles like sunshine, and hearts open wide,
We share in the laughter, our whimsical ride.

The Dance of Existence

Life's a grand party, a whimsical ball,
Where the jester's our guide, and we all heed the call.
With each step we're flipping, and twirling around,
In this silly old dance, it's joy that we've found.

The music is quirky, a tune made of glee,
As we laugh at ourselves, so wild and so free.
In this merry whirl, let's not take a fall,
For the dance of existence is the best game of all.

Witty Reflections

Mirrors show faces, some funny, some bright,
With grins that can spark joy, like stars born of light.
We jest with our shadows, in playful embrace,
Finding humor in flaws, a warm, loving space.

Each wrinkle a story, a chuckle to share,
In the gallery of life, we're all art laid bare.
With every cracked smile, a reflection we find,
That the best kind of wisdom is born from the mind.

Chasing Shadows and Sunbeams

We chase after shadows, like kids on a spree,
With giggles that echo, so wild and so free.
Sunbeams are jokers, they dance and they tease,
Casting silliness down, as they flutter with ease.

The world is a circus, with laughter in tow,
As we tumble and trip, with nowhere to go.
In this game of delight, where whimsy is king,
Let's savor each moment, and joyfully sing.

The Playful Dance of Destiny

In a world where jesters twirl,
The sun wears a floppy hat,
Dancing cats and a whirling pearl,
Chasing shadows, quick and sprat.

Life's a game with cards that tease,
Jackpot jokes and silly tricks,
The breeze whispers with a sneeze,
Tickled hearts in rhythm mix.

With a leap and bound we play,
Chasing dreams that wave and dart,
Every mishap lights the way,
The punchline found within the heart.

So let us waltz on fate's own floor,
Where seriousness takes a nap,
With laughter's echo forevermore,
This jestful journey is the map.

Glee in the Grayscale

In a world of shadows bleak,
Where colors fade and spirits frown,
A tiny mouse begins to speak,
Spinning tales that wear the crown.

With pockets stuffed full of cheese,
He prances on the paper gray,
Each nibble brings a sense of ease,
Brightening up the dullest day.

As clocks tick backwards, time does play,
The moonlight giggles on the roof,
In grayscale life, we find a way,
To turn the sordid into proof.

So wear your mismatched socks with pride,
Dance in puddles, shout with glee,
For in the gray we'll often glide,
Embracing every sight we see.

The Parody of Purpose

In a world where fish can fly,
And cows recite the news at dawn,
We ponder now just by and by,
As chaos reigns and rules are drawn.

With a pickle suit and hat askew,
We prance on paths of peanut fudge,
Every aim leads us askew,
In laughter's arms, we do not budge.

Questions hang like jellybeans,
While answers bounce like rubber ducks,
Purpose hides behind the scenes,
With giggles mixed in our good lucks.

So let us prance in silly guise,
With playful thoughts that never cease,
In parody, the truest prize,
Is finding joy and simple peace.

Snickers at the Universe's Scheme

Beneath the stars, a wise old cat,
Reviews the jokes of cosmic lore,
With cosmic yarn and a feathered hat,
He winks and gives a feline roar.

Each planet spins in playful jest,
Around the sun, they twirl like pie,
Comets chuckle, they're not stressed,
As worlds collide and giggles fly.

In the vastness, a cosmic wink,
The universe just loves to tease,
Each blink evokes a curious blink,
As we partake in silly breeze.

So take a seat, enjoy the show,
In the grand play of space and time,
With every wisp and little glow,
The scheme unfolds, like silly rhyme.

Chasing Chuckles in the Dark

In shadows where the giggles creep,
A sneeze may wake the silence deep.
With silly faces, we play charades,
As moonlight dances, laughter cascades.

Tangled tales and playful pranks,
Whiskers twitch at secret banks.
The clock ticks loud but we don't mind,
In this hushed world, joy's redefined.

Footsteps echo, a playful race,
Time stands still in this shared space.
With every blink, a new absurd,
In quirky moments, truth's inferred.

So here we roam, in jest we find,
The silly threads that life has twined.
With hearts so light, we dare to spark,
Eternal giggles in the dark.

Beneath the Surface, Laughter Blooms

In puddles shallow, smiles will splash,
A hearty laugh, a lightning flash.
With every cloud that drifts above,
A little joke, a burst of love.

Beneath the moody skies so grey,
A chuckle waits, not far away.
With every sigh, a story's spun,
A timeless jest, our hearts have won.

Oceans of woes may swell and churn,
Yet in the tide, sweet jest we learn.
For life's absurd, yet oh so bright,
We find the joy in day and night.

So let's dive deep and uncover glee,
In silly depths, we'll float carefree.
In every wave, a giggle looms,
And from the dark, our laughter blooms.

Sunbeams and Sardonic Smiles

Chasing sunbeams on a whim,
With cocked eyebrows, we grin and swim.
In the warmth of rays, we tease and play,
Finding joy in the smirk of the day.

Coffee spills and dogs that bark,
Mistaken steps that leave a mark.
With silly faces, a comical guise,
In everyday life, magic lies.

As shadows stretch, the evening hums,
With every clatter, laughter drums.
In winks exchanged, we understand,
The charm of mischief, always grand.

So let's toast to the quirks we find,
In every moment, life's unrefined.
With sunbeams wrapped and smiles beguiled,
We dance through life, forever wild.

Revelry in the Ordinary

On starlit nights, we stake our claim,
In kitchen chaos, we find our fame.
With spatulas raised, we fight the dough,
In epic battles, side by side, we glow.

The laundry spins, the dishes sing,
In silly notes, our hearts take wing.
With every task, a jest we weave,
In simple acts, the joy we believe.

As morning brews a caffeinated dream,
A wink exchanged, oh, how we beam!
In ordinary wears, the magic grows,
In playful antics, little glows.

So let's dance through the mundane, dear,
With each shared laugh, we persevere.
In everyday revels, we'll always see,
That joy is found in you and me.

The Luminescence of Laughter

When clumsy feet meet slippery floors,
We tumble and glide through opened doors.
A giggle echoes 'neath a starry night,
Embracing chaos, oh what a sight!

With socks that clash and shoes untied,
We waddle forth, no need to hide.
Life's little mishaps bring us cheer,
In silly moments, joy draws near.

The world's a joke, a grand charade,
With puns and pouts, we serenade.
In every blunder, wisdom's spun,
We sip the nectar of silly fun.

So raise your glass to the clumsy grace,
To laughter's charm in this wild race.
For every slip is a tale retold,
In the dance of laughter, life unfolds.

Dance of Delightful Dilemmas

Oh, what a toss when socks collide,
One's blue and bright, the other's wide.
Fate's a jester with tricks in hand,
In the circus of choices, we take a stand.

The stew's too salty, the cake won't rise,
Yet we feast on giggles, oh what a prize!
With every puzzle, we twist and shout,
Life's quirky riddles, we can't live without.

When plans go awry and time disappears,
We spin in circles, squashing our fears.
With smiles on lips, we create our fate,
In the dance of dilemmas, we celebrate.

So pirouette through fears you've fought,
Embrace the mayhem that joy has brought.
For each wrong turn is a ticket to glee,
In this playful waltz, we're forever free.

The Magic of Mundanity

A simple cup of morning brew,
Turns mundane moments into something new.
We toast to crumbs on the kitchen floor,
And laugh at life's little uproar.

With mismatched socks and a lopsided hat,
We strut through life, just imagine that!
For every trip and every spill,
Hides a spark of joy, an uncharted thrill.

In cracks on the pavement, wisdom hides,
Beckoning smiles where the silliness abides.
With a wink at chores that never cease,
We dance through dullness, finding our peace.

So cherish the chaos, embrace the plain,
In weekly rituals, there's laughter to gain.
For magic lives in the ordinary scene,
Where joy ignites and laughter reigns.

The Jolly Journey

Beneath the stars, our mishaps gleam,
We stumble and trip, fueling the dream.
With each new laugh, our spirits grow,
In the comedy of life, we steal the show.

With backpacks stuffed and maps askew,
Adventure's spark ignites anew.
We'll ride the waves on wobbling boats,
And sing our hearts out with silly notes.

When plans go south and moments flop,
We chase the chuckles, we never stop.
With open hearts and restless feet,
This jolly journey can't be beat.

So let's skip stones and chase the breeze,
With giggles that dance among the trees.
In this travelogue through laughs and cheer,
Life's jolly journey is so sincere.

Jests in the Journey

Life's a circus, full of jest,
With clowns and tricks, we must invest.
A whoopee cushion on a chair,
Turns solemn sights to laughter's air.

In puddles deep, we take a leap,
With rubber boots, we make a sweep.
The sprinkle turns to giggle storms,
As joy reform, the heart adorns.

A banana slip in running race,
Shows that we stumble in our pace.
Yet every trip, a chance to shine,
We jive and jolt—our spirits align.

So raise a glass to silly quirks,
Embrace the dance of oddball perks.
For in this ride, we find the clue,
Life's a jest, and we're the crew.

The Comedy of Shadows

Shadows stretch in playful chase,
Twisting forms, a mischievous grace.
A cat that leaps, then slips and slides,
In giggles pure, the shadow abides.

With every prank that daylight brings,
A voice of laughter softly sings.
The sun sets low, the jokes ignite,
As shadows dance with sheer delight.

A tree that leans to share a grin,
Winks at the world, lets fun begin.
And every dusk that creeps anew,
Whispers tales in hues of blue.

So let us find in evening's shroud,
The humor soft, the laughter loud.
For shadows play as we indulge,
In the comedy where dreams divulge.

Smiles in the Storm

When clouds roll in with rumbling might,
   We dance in puddles, hearts alight.
   Each raindrop sings a playful tune,
   As lightning snaps a grinning moon.

   Umbrellas flipped, a mighty flight,
     A paper boat in squishy plight.
   We laugh at winds that twist and twirl,
     As nature chuckles, life un-furl.

     In every gust, a chance to play,
   With splashes bright, we greet the day.
     A thunderclap, a joyful shout,
   In storms, we find what life's about.

So while the skies may weep and wail,
   We wrap ourselves in whimsy's veil.
   With smiles wide, we brave the storm,
     And find a joke in every form.

Winking at the Cosmos

Stars above in playful wink,
Invite us all to stop and think.
The cosmos giggles, oh so bright,
With tales of mysteries in the night.

A comet zips, a cheeky grin,
As planets bounce, let the fun begin.
Galaxies swirl in joyous dance,
Encouraging each soul to take a chance.

The universe whispers, "Don't be dull,
Embrace the whimsy, feel the pull."
A black hole teases with a pout,
As cosmic jokes are spun about.

So here we stand, beneath the skies,
With laughter echoing, love replies.
In every twinkle, find your cheer,
For life's a jest, and joy is near.

Mirth in the Midst of Meaning

Amidst the chaos, smiles break free,
Jokes dance lightly, like a bumblebee.
Life's a riddle, wrapped up tight,
With giggles as the guiding light.

We stumble forward, tripping often,
In the absurd, our hearts are soften.
Tickles in our tummies, what a delight,
Finding joy in the silliest sight.

With quirks and questions, we prance about,
Not a clue, yet we cheer and shout.
In whimsy's embrace, we take a leap,
The puzzle's charm lulls us to sleep.

Each twist and turn, a secret surprise,
Through laughter's door, life's magic lies.
For in the jokes and playful jest,
We find our truth, we find our best.

The Art of Smirking at Fate

Life throws curveballs, straight at my head,
But with a wink, I laugh instead.
A jester's cap, my crown of cheer,
In folly's court, I will not fear.

With jigs and jives, I'll dance along,
Fate's silly tune, a merry song.
When trouble knocks, I'll simply prance,
In the clumsy steps of fate's own dance.

Every mishap's just a fun-filled scene,
A playful poke from the unseen.
With smiles that tickle and grins so wide,
I stroll through chaos, with joy as my guide.

So here's to whimsy, the heart's sweet jest,
For in the laughter, I find my rest.
When life gets strange, I just smirk and sway,
With humor's glow, I'll brighten the day.

Whimsy Weaved into Reality

Threads of laughter, woven bright,
In the fabric of day, they bring delight.
With twinkles in eyes and puns in store,
We paint our lives, and then some more.

A sprinkle of mischief, a splash of glee,
In the dance of life, we twirl so free.
Silly hats and goofy shoes,
In the game of chance, we cannot lose.

We chase the clouds and tickle the breeze,
In the heart of jest, we find our ease.
The world's a stage, absurd and grand,
Where every laughter is carefully planned.

With quirks and giggles, we roam the night,
Filling the dark with our inner light.
Reality bends, loses its grip,
When joy leads off on another trip.

Silliness at the Summit

At the peak of life, where shadows play,
Silliness reigns, come what may.
With silly smiles and lightened loads,
We scale the heights and bounce on roads.

Giggling down slopes, we tumble and roll,
Finding surprise in every hole.
With each little slip, a hearty cheer,
We dance with fate, make the worries clear.

Bizarre and bright, this view so wide,
With chuckles and jests, we take pride.
As the clouds drift by, we claim our space,
In this joyful realm, we quicken the pace.

So raise your glass to absurdity's call,
In the summit's laughter, we'll never fall.
For life's a joke, a playful tease,
In the peaks of joy, we find our ease.

Giggles in the Gloom

When clouds hang low, and shadows creep,
We find the joy in secrets we keep.
A tickle here, a chuckle there,
Brightens the day, lifts the despair.

With every frown that tries to stay,
A silly dance will chase it away.
Slip on a banana, tumble with glee,
Life's best moments are free as can be.

Humor as a Companion

A wink and a smile, the world's in play,
Turning troubles into yarns that sway.
Join in the jest, let worries unwind,
In laughter's embrace, peace we find.

Knock-knock jokes at the break of dawn,
Who knew the day would promise a brawn?
Quirky, yet lovely, our lives intertwine,
Shared giggles reveal how sweet we shine.

Echoed Exuberance

With every hiccup, a joke takes flight,
In silly tales, darkness turns bright.
Puns in the air, like bubbles we blow,
Making a splash, even in woe.

Chasing the blues with antics anew,
Tails of mishaps, the joyful crew.
We snicker at fate, with a gleam in our eyes,
Each hearty chuckle a clever disguise.

The Festival of Follies

Party hats and colorful socks,
Stumbling over made-up blocks.
A whimsical joust on the lawn today,
Where laughter reigns, and fears decay.

Silly games and pie in the face,
Chaos ignites, but we still embrace.
With every twist, our hearts take flight,
A carnival of giggles, pure delight.

Epiphanies in Exaggeration

In a world where cats can drive,
And pickles dance, they come alive.
A talking shoe with quite the tale,
Sails on dreams, a starship's trail.

Lemonade flows from the skies,
As squirrels wear hats, oh what a surprise!
Socks in pairs engage in a fight,
While sleepy clouds snore through the night.

A dog reads books in a silly pose,
While jellybeans perform their shows.
The sun winks as it sips on tea,
A circus of joy, wild and free.

So here we are, in moments grand,
Where giggles are treasures, oh so well planned.
With every twist, let laughter ignite,
In epiphanies where whimsy takes flight.

The Serenade of Snickers

Beneath the moon, a frog does croon,
Its voice a tune that makes us swoon.
With pink guitars, the stars join in,
And fireflies chuckle, where dreams begin.

A cupcake winks at a chocolate pie,
As spaghetti dreams of learning to fly.
The audience? A crew of giggling mice,
Feasting on cake crumbs, a true paradise.

In the garden, where jokes grow tall,
The daisies whisper a playful call.
With rhymes that tickle the funny bone,
Each line a treasure, each chuckle, our own.

So let us dance with smiles so bright,
Join the serenade, take flight tonight.
With snickers echoing, pure delight,
In this land of quirks, everything feels right.

Witty Whirlwinds

A whirlwind spins with a silly grin,
As gumdrops tumble, let the fun begin.
Windows shake to kites that sing,
A symphony of nonsense, joy they bring.

Captain Rabbit sails on a boat of cheese,
While beanbag chairs float with the breeze.
The clouds above wear polka-dot hats,
As laughter erupts with giggling spats.

Funny hats march down the street,
Twirling on toes to a jolly beat.
Lemon slices play hopscotch bright,
While marshmallows plan a comedy night.

So whirl with me in this dance of jest,
In witty winds, we'll find our quest.
For life's a party, never shy,
With playful spirits that kiss the sky.

Nimbus of Nonsense

On a cloud made of whipped cream and dreams,
A sea of jelly flows in sillier streams.
The sun dives under a purple sea,
While giggly giraffes sip iced tea.

A penguin juggles fish in the air,
While a cactus dons a ballooning flair.
The world spins wild, in colors so bright,
In the nimbus of nonsense, we take flight.

Cotton candy trees sway with delight,
As rubber ducks race in pure moonlight.
Every rib-tickling twist and shout,
Turns life's routine inside out.

So join this circus of pure delight,
Where goofy giggles chase away fright.
In the clouds of whimsy, we'll play the game,
And find joy where nonsense holds no shame.

Sparkling Ironies

In a world of twists and grins,
Where wisdom wears mismatched socks,
A jester juggles all our sins,
While time ticks by like silly clocks.

A cat who thinks it's in control,
Turns to chase its own long tail,
Amidst the chaos, we find soul,
In every wobbly, wild tale.

We chase our dreams on rainbow trails,
With cups of tea and silly hats,
While up above, the stork prevails,
Delivering laughs with little spats.

So let us dance in life's parade,
With every stumble, every cheer,
For in this play, we're all arrayed,
To find the joy in every tear.

The Jestful Path

Beneath the clouds of cotton candy,
Where folks wear shoes that squeak and slide,
We wander paths that twist unhandy,
With echoes of our joys inside.

A pickle jar can start a chat,
With thoughts exchanged like bouncing balls,
We giggle at the irony that
A trip to town means shopping malls.

In mirrors where the faces dance,
Reflections spark with cheeky looks,
Each fumble gives a second chance,
And life's a plot with silly books.

So throw your doubts into the air,
With feet that tap on hope's warm ground,
Embrace the world, in laughter share,
As joy is where our hearts are found.

Life's Lighthearted Labyrinth

Wandering through this maze of fun,
Where jokes jump out like hidden doors,
We chase the sunshine, on the run,
And often find what laughter stores.

A squirrel wearing tiny boots,
Dances on branches, acorn dream,
As life unfolds in silly shoots,
Like jokes that flow in playful stream.

Each step we take is filled with cheer,
As grins unwrap like gifts that sing,
In corridors of hope, we steer,
To greet the oddities life brings.

So spin around and join the show,
With every twist that turns our way,
For in this game of high and low,
We find the spark, we find the play.

Chronicles of Cheer

In tales of yore, where jesters played,
Their antics spun a web of bliss,
They painted smiles where woes arrayed,
With every poke and silly kiss.

The moon, a face with winks galore,
Watches over our fumbles bright,
And every starlit night restores,
The tales that tickle us with light.

We scribble notes in laughter's ink,
On moments lost and moments found,
In every blink, we pause and think,
That joyful hearts are tightly bound.

So gather 'round, our stories told,
In every laugh, a truth appears,
With quirks and quirks, life's treasures unfold,
As we find cheer beneath our fears.

A Palette of Playfulness

In a world where shadows dance,
Colors burst, given a chance.
Tickled pink, we swirl and sway,
Life's a jest, come join the play.

Spinning tales of mishaps grand,
With each slip, we understand.
Giggles bubbling like a spring,
Every blunder makes us sing.

Chasing rainbows, we find glee,
In every turn, a mystery.
Brush our worries with a grin,
In this canvas, we'll begin.

So dip your toes in joy today,
Let's color life, come what may.
With every laugh, our hearts ignite,
Creating art with pure delight.

The Quip of the Cosmos

Stars wink down, a cosmic joke,
Planets spin as comets poke.
Galaxies giggle in their play,
Universal laughs light the way.

A black hole swallows, what a sight,
Sucking in all, with delight.
Time's a trickster, what a clown,
Wormholes flip us upside down.

Gravity pulls us, what a tease,
Astronauts float with such great ease.
In orbit's arms, we twirl and spin,
The universe chuckles from within.

So when you ponder, look above,
The night sky twinkles with its love.
In laughter's echo, we discover,
The cosmos winks at every blunder.

Ticklish Truths

Life's a riddle wrapped in fun,
With every tick, and every pun.
Truths are sly, hiding with grace,
Tickling hearts in every space.

When plans go south, we bend and turn,
In every stumble, lessons learn.
A guffaw here, a chuckle there,
Finding joy, beyond compare.

Surprises lurk behind each door,
An unexpected encore.
With every hiccup, life reveals,
Glimpses of how laughter heals.

So let's embrace this whimsy spree,
Ticklish truths that set us free.
Smiles to share, and tales to weave,
In the joy of life, we believe.

Lively Musings

In a café, stories brew,
Laughter spills like morning dew.
With every sip, we toast to cheer,
Lively musings draw us near.

Jokes abound on every wall,
Sprinkles of joy, hear the call.
A wink, a nod, the world's a stage,
In this dance, we disengage.

Life's a game of hide and seek,
Funny faces, all unique.
Embrace the silly, let it shine,
In every moment, make it divine.

So raise your cup, toast the absurd,
In everyday whimsy, hope's conferred.
With hearty laughs, our spirits lift,
In the tapestry of joy, we shift.

Silliness and Substance

A jester dances in a bowl,
Twirling spoons and spouting soul.
With every wink, the world takes flight,
Whimsy turns the dark to bright.

In puddles deep, a splashy cheer,
Rubber ducks that float so near.
Life's recipe calls for a dash,
Of giggles caught in moments flash.

A clumsy mime, he trips and falls,
Whispers echo through chapel halls.
Each snicker sings like birds in trees,
Joy disguised as a playful breeze.

Lost in jest, we find our way,
Chasing shadows of the day.
For every frown or heavy sigh,
There's a grin that's waiting by.

Smirks in the Shadows

In corners dark where secrets hide,
A smirk emerges, wise and wide.
It chuckles deep, a whispered tune,
  Dancing lightly 'neath the moon.

A cat appears, with eyes aglow,
Slinking through life, just moving slow.
It plays with yarn and pounces low,
  Each purr a joke that's sure to flow.

The clock ticks loud, but we don't care,
  As time slips by in a funny glare.
With every tick, a punchline strikes,
  Life's comedy, just like our likes.

In every crevice, joy does creep,
In shadows where the sillies leap.
So when you think the woes come round,
  Remember, laughter's always found.

The Heart's Secret Laughter

In quiet rooms where echoes play,
The heart, it giggles, come what may.
Each tender beat and whispered sigh,
Tickles memories, oh so spry.

Beneath the masks that life has drawn,
Witty sparks of joy live on.
A wink, a grin, a gentle tease,
Unraveling the knots with ease.

Balloons of dreams float high and bright,
Chasing whims into the night.
A secret laugh inside your chest,
Reminds us all to jest and jest.

A playful heart, its song's mischief,
Paints the world in shades of bliss.
For every tear, a chuckle's near,
Life's greatest joke, let's hold it dear.

Lightness Among Life's Burdens

A heavy load, we all must bear,
But there's a sprite that fills the air.
With merry jiggles, giggles bright,
It lifts the weight with sheer delight.

A jumbled mind, a brain so wild,
Crafting tales just like a child.
In every mishap, there's a spark,
Turning troubles into art.

The broken chair, the coffee spill,
Such moments weave a funny thrill.
For in each slip upon the floor,
Lies laughter waiting at the door.

So toss the burden, take a chance,
Join in the light and silly dance.
In life's grand circus, take a bow,
For happiness is here, right now.

Giggles in the Gloom

In a world that seems to frown,
We find the jests to turn it around.
Tickles in every corner we see,
Laughter, the key to feeling free.

When clouds hang thick and gray,
We dance in puddles, come what may.
With every step, a snicker penned,
In the gloom, the fun won't end.

Frogs in tuxedos join the show,
Their leaping antics steal the glow.
A silly charade begins to sway,
Who knew gloom could lead to play?

So here we stand, a merry bunch,
With every giggle, we pack a punch.
In the funhouse of our dreams we dive,
Finding joy means we're truly alive.

Whispers of Joy Amidst Shadows

In the dark where whispers play,
Shadows giggle at the end of day.
Each corner holds a secret jest,
In the quiet, we are blessed.

Midnight snacks and silly sighs,
The moonlight catches our playful eyes.
When troubles come, we share a grin,
In our world, there's laughter within.

Footsteps echo with a twist,
A dance of joy that can't be missed.
Who knew shadows could beam so bright?
They tickle our hearts, making it light.

With every low, we raise our cheer,
In the face of doubt, we persevere.
Whispers of joy, soft and sweet,
Bring the shadows to our feet.

The Humor of Existence

Life's a riddle, wrapped in tape,
A puppy dressed as a superhero cape.
The ups and downs are quite the ride,
With humor as our trusty guide.

A bird on a wire, sings out loud,
Mocking the traffic, so unbowed.
Every mishap becomes a song,
In the chaos, we know we belong.

Socks that dance while you're asleep,
Are proof that laughter's ours to keep.
Existence teeters on a line,
Where jokes and joy perfectly entwine.

Like a clown in a serious suit,
Life's punchlines make our hearts salute.
In each odd twist that we parade,
The humor of existence will never fade.

Grins Beneath the Weight of Stars

Beneath the cosmos, glimmers bright,
We trade our worries for sheer delight.
With twinkling eyes and open hearts,
We spin our dreams, crafting arts.

Among the planets, we tell our tales,
Of goofy dreams and epic fails.
Stars winking down with a knowing glow,
Remind us the best jest is to let go.

On cosmic waves, we surf and play,
Counting comets on a breezy day.
With every chuckle, we lighten the load,
Turning the universe into a fun abode.

So here's to grins, no matter the scale,
Building a joy that'll never pale.
Underneath those twinkling guides,
We find the magic where laughter hides.

Grateful Guffaws

In a world so bright, we trip and fall,
With every stumble, we hear the call.
Life's a jester, playing his trick,
Smiles emerge, our joy to pick.

Tickles of fate, they come in waves,
With silly quirks, we all behave.
Each tiny hiccup, a spark of cheer,
We dance with joy, the jesters near.

In wrinkles of time, laughter grows wide,
Embrace the quirks, take them in stride.
For every fumble, there's a delight,
As giggles bloom in the soft moonlight.

So let us cheer for the ups and downs,
In the carnival of the silly clowns.
With hearts so light, we ride the wave,
Grateful guffaws, our souls to save.

The Comics of Our Lives

Every morning, the sun cracks a smile,
Life's a comic, let's read for a while.
With panels of joy, and frames of fun,
We giggle and chuckle, until the day's done.

Characters dance in zany delight,
Chasing their tails, from morning till night.
A mishap here, a charm gone rogue,
Creation's a mess, but we're in the vogue.

With laughter lines drawn, the story unfolds,
In a world of whimsy, bright and bold.
Comics and anecdotes make us believe,
That joy's the punchline we all can weave.

So grab the pen, draw your tale anew,
In the sketches of life, find humor too.
As every blunder colors our way,
Together we'll laugh through the fray!

Winks from the Universe

The stars above wink, a celestial jest,
Life's a game, put humor to the test.
In cosmic chuckles, the galaxies grin,
Finding joy in the chaos we're in.

Each day a riddle, a quirky surprise,
The universe smirks, oh how it flies!
With planets in motion, they spin and sway,
We giggle along, come what may.

A comet zooms by with a playful cheer,
Whispers of joy drip down from the sphere.
As moonbeams giggle, lighting our fears,
The universe winks; let laughter endear.

In this whimsical dance, we all play a part,
Each tickle of fate, a gift to the heart.
With every hiccup, we learn to embrace,
The winks from above, a joyful place.

Enigmas and Giggles

In the puzzle of life, each piece is wild,
An enigma wrapped in laughter, like a child.
With every question, a chuckle springs,
Life's funny riddles, such curious things.

Jokes hidden deep in the everyday grind,
Searching for clues, let humor unwind.
A wink from the cat, a sly little gaze,
In absurdity, we'll find our ways.

Fractured timelines and quirky twists,
Unraveling laughs from life's gentle lists.
In the midst of the chaos, giggles arise,
Turning the serious into surprise.

So here we stand, amidst giggles and grins,
Collecting the moments, where laughter begins.
With enigmas to crack, and jokes to ignite,
We flourish together, dancing in light.

Cheerful Chaos of Being

In a world of silly twists,
We trip on what we thought was bliss.
A banana peel, a wobbly chair,
Life's a dance, if we just dare.

The cat thinks it's a ninja fierce,
A leap in air, then a quick pierce.
We giggle at the tangled threads,
As all our serious plans just spread.

With socks that clash and hair in knots,
We stroll through life, collecting thoughts.
A toilet roll held high in pride,
Who knew such fun, we'd have, we'd bide?

So let's embrace the silly ways,
And count our quirks as joyful rays.
For in the chaos, laughter glows,
A carousel of highs and lows.

The Comic Relief of Creation

In the kitchen, pots collide,
As spatulas take a wild ride.
Flour flies like winter's snow,
A delicious mess, with a bright glow.

The sun and moon play hide and seek,
While clouds join in, feeling cheeky.
They bounce and roll, a game in sight,
Even stars sparkle with delight.

The trees whisper jokes in the breeze,
While nature chuckles with such ease.
A frog in shoes jumps on a whim,
And life's a stage with a silly spin.

So let us toast with mugs held high,
To absurd moments that we can't deny.
For in this cosmic comedy,
Each twist reveals our jubilee.

Playful Ponderings

What if the moon wore polka dots?
And aliens bake with burning pots?
Imagining worlds, oh so absurd,
A zany thought, not to be deterred.

A penguin waltzes on a grill,
Chasing dreams with a comical thrill.
The daisies gossip, wearing crowns,
As bees buzz by with laughter sounds.

If socks had thoughts, what tales they'd weave,
Of lost match-ups and autumn leaves!
A rubber duck debates with a whale,
On best escape routes, with a squeaky trail.

So ponder while you wander wide,
In this fantastic, playful ride.
For every silly thought you chase,
Reminds us all, life's a jolly race.

Revelations in Laughter

Behind closed doors, we let it out,
A snort, a giggle, then a shout.
Each secret shared becomes a jest,
And in that moment, we feel blessed.

The old dog dreams of flying high,
While neighbors wonder why he'll try.
A rocket ship made of cookie dough,
We aim for stars, not fear the low.

And when the clock ticks loud and fast,
We pause and make the moment last.
With punchlines ready, hearts set free,
As silly thoughts float joyfully.

So let us treasure every grin,
For in each chuckle, joy begins.
Together we'll find that silly spark,
As life's a laugh in light and dark.

Cheer in the Clutter

In a room full of jumble, I dance with a sock,
The dog finds my shoe and gives it a shock.
Forgotten old treasures, stacked high on a shelf,
I trip on a box, oh how I amuse myself.

A spoon in the fridge, what a curious sight,
I guess it was Sunday; the fridge took a bite.
With giggles and gaffes, I twirl in the mess,
Each noodle and tidbit, a joyous excess.

Atop all this chaos, a cat starts to leap,
Knocking down papers—it's poetry deep!
The laughter erupts, as I can't help but grin,
In this clutter of life, let the fun just begin.

So gather the chaos, and hold it so tight,
In the whimsy of clutter, we find pure delight.
With chocolate and giggles, we savor the day,
Finding joy in the madness, come what may.

Mischief and Meaning

With a wink and a grin, we plot all the schemes,
Like raindrops on rooftops, we dance in our dreams.
The pickles and jelly, a sandwich gone wild,
Life's sweet surprises, just like a young child.

Whispers in shadows, each giggle we share,
The world turns absurd, but who really cares?
Walking on rooftops, we dance on the edge,
Chasing our laughter, we pledge, we allege.

The cat on the counter, a thief in the night,
Makes off with the cupcake, all frosted and bright.
With sprinkles and shenanigans, stories unfold,
Each moment a treasure, worth more than pure gold.

So swing from the chandeliers, let mischief take flight,
In the dance of the day, everything feels right.
With each silly act, we find joy in the seam,
As meaning is painted with laughter's sweet beam.

The Lightness of Being

A bubble of laughter floats high in the air,
While socks go on strike—they're a comical pair.
A head full of dreams, but shoes on the ground,
Floating on clouds, or spinning around.

With twirls in the kitchen, I'm mixing my brew,
A dash of pure silliness adds something new.
The cakes laugh and rise, as if in a play,
In the circus of baking, I lose track of day.

The coffee's a jester, with beans full of cheer,
Each sip feels like sunshine, brightening up here.
A dance in the morning, I trip on the rug,
And find all my slippers give each other a hug.

So let's toast to the small things, the giggles, the fun,
In the lightness of being, we dance with the sun.
With joy as our compass, we'll roam with a tune,
And savor each moment, from morning to moon.

Mirthful Mysteries

In a land of odd puzzles, I stumble and trip,
A spoon in the mirror, it's quite a strange grip.
The socks play a game of hide-and-seek,
As giggles spill softly, they playfully squeak.

A pen turns to paper, a dance on the desk,
Words swirl like confetti, both wild and grotesque.
When bananas start singing, oh what could that mean?
Is life just a joke with a whimsical sheen?

The cats form a committee, all plotting a heist,
To snatch away dinner, an ambitious little feist.
In the circus of living, smiles burst like a cheer,
With mysteries wrapped in laughter so near.

So come join the shenanigans, let the joy unfold,
In the mirthful mysteries, bright stories are told.
Every giggle a riddle, we chase with delight,
In this tapestry woven with laughter's pure light.

The Quirk of Creation

In a world full of quirks and charms,
Laughter dances like sweet alarms.
Every fumble, every fall,
Is just life's way of having a ball.

Mismatched socks, a silly hat,
The universe grins under the mat.
With each blunder, wisdom gained,
All the worry seems so far drained.

Clouds might giggle, raindrops tease,
Nature's jokes come with such ease.
From silly squirrels to bouncy bees,
Life's punchline floats upon the breeze.

So let's embrace the weird and wild,
With every chuckle, we're beguiled.
For in this riddle, so divine,
The joy's in jest, and all is fine.

Bright Side of Brevity

A fleeting glance, a wink, a grin,
The short and sweet moments begin.
A whispered joke, a playful tease,
In simple lines, our hearts find ease.

The punchline lands with hardly a press,
A hop, a skip, a moment's jest.
In every tick that may seem slight,
There lies a spark, a pure delight.

Tiny tales that swirl and spin,
Catch us laughing from within.
Short and snappy, light and bright,
Life's essence shines in purest light.

Even the stars, in their brief twinkles,
Giggle softly, spark like sprinkles.
In brevity, the wisdom rolls,
As humor livens weary souls.

Chuckles in the Chaos

Amidst the rush, the daily grind,
A smirk appears, so well-designed.
Traffic jams, the world's a stage,
In chaos, wit bursts from a cage.

A toddler's spill, a dog that prances,
Life's wild rhythms hold their chances.
Every trip, a story told,
In the jumbled mess, some gold.

Pie charts, graphs, and to-do lists,
All of life's little twists and trysts.
With every twisty, bumpy ride,
A laugh appears, we cannot hide.

So take a seat, and roll with glee,
In rocky paths, there's harmony.
For in the storm, the smiles burst,
In chaos, laughter quenches thirst.

The Humor in Heartbeats

Every heartbeat, a playful thump,
Life's tempo guides us with a jump.
A rhythm of joy, with skips and hops,
In the dance of days, the laughter pops.

Ticklish moments, a tick and tock,
In gentle nudges, life plays its clock.
The silly sounds, a giddy cheer,
With every pulse, the joy draws near.

From whispered jokes to a raucous roar,
Each heartbeat sings what we adore.
With every breath, in sync we sway,
Discovering humor in every day.

So feel the pings within your chest,
In every laugh, we find our zest.
Life's heartbeat is a funny song,
In this odd dance, we all belong.

Joy Between the Lines

In the margins of our day,
We scribble things that sway.
A coffee spill, a cat that sits,
Life's a joke with little bits.

The tickle of a sunny breeze,
Dancing shadows through the trees.
We slip on paths of silly sighs,
With laughter spilling from our eyes.

A squirrel dressed in a tiny hat,
Takes a leap and falls like that!
We giggle at the way we fall,
Life's a whimsy, don't you call?

So raise a cup, toast to the fun,
Under the bright and warming sun.
For in our quirks, joy we find,
A hearty laugh, our hearts aligned.

Carousels of Cosmic Chuckles

Round and round we twirl with glee,
On a ride of pure jubilee.
The stars wink with a playful grin,
As we spin and spin and spin.

From jellybeans to soaring kites,
The universe shares its delights.
In every corner, joy resides,
In silly antics life abides.

Wobbly feet on roller skates,
A jester hops, while laughter waits.
The cosmos plays a playful game,
With twists and turns, it's never lame.

So join the dance, no need to ask,
In this grand and joyful task.
For every giggle, every cheer,
In cosmic chuckles, we persevere.

The Laughter that Echoes

Beneath the trees, a secret calls,
Where laughter bounces off the walls.
A pebble tossed, a splash of joy,
Childlike wonder, still no ploy.

Whispers ride the gentle breeze,
To tickle thoughts with utmost ease.
The world's a stage, and we're the show,
With punchlines hidden in the flow.

Each stumble met with light applause,
A playful "oops" becomes our cause.
In echo chambers of delight,
We find the day turns into night.

So hear the laughter echo loud,
Merge your smile into the crowd.
For in each moment, joy will lend,
A merry heart that will not end.

Quirks of Existence

A pancake flip, a syrup spill,
A toddler's laugh, a belly's thrill.
Life's strange quirks, from big to small,
In every moment, let's stand tall.

Umbrellas flipped in sudden rain,
A dance with puddles, oh, the gain!
We watch a dog chase its own tail,
In simple joys, we shall not fail.

Curly straws and goofy hats,
Life's a circus, imagine that!
With a wink and a solid grin,
Each quirk invites the child within.

So join the fun, don't hesitate,
In whimsical joys, we celebrate.
For laughter lingers in the air,
In quirks of life, we find our share.

Cheerful Cataclysms

In a world so full of blunders,
A cat slipped on banana peels,
Frogs singing off-key wonders,
   And everyone just reels.

Hats blown by the wind's still fate,
A dog wears sunglasses with style,
We dance to missteps that create,
   Joy bursting out for a while.

Spilled soup turns into a game,
As noodles twist like a swagger,
Oh, who could ever feel the same,
When chaos shows up with a stagger?

Through silly trips and leaps we find,
That life's a stage, a jest, a play,
With laughter painted on the mind,
   In every goofy, wild array.

The Symphony of Smiles

The toaster popped a tune so bright,
While cereal danced in the bowl,
Milk splashed high, what a delightful sight,
As music filled up the soul.

Birds tweeting like they're in a band,
With squirrels who keep on the beat,
It's nature's groove, wonderfully planned,
A chaotic, yet tasty treat.

Grasshoppers tap-dance on the lawn,
The sun grins wide in the sky,
Each giggle a flower that's drawn,
In the garden where joy is nigh.

With every chuckle, the world spins round,
Creating a melody of glee,
A symphony in which we are bound,
In the laughter we all can see.

Revelations and Revelry

A light bulb flickers with a grin,
As socks mate in a laundry spree,
What a joy when chaos begins,
    In this cosmic jubilee.

We find a dance in every stumble,
And tickle fights with every fall,
Life's mysteries in giggles tumble,
Oh, how we embrace them all!

Candles flicker, cakes start to spin,
While sprinkles sprinkle a tale,
In moments where we just dive in,
Paint our troubles with a veil.

Each revelation brings us cheer,
As jokes unfold and stories blend,
Let's raise a glass, let's toast the year,
For laughter is the truest friend.

Jests of the Journey

On a path that twists and twirls,
A tumbleweed blows past my shoe,
Life's a puzzle, full of swirls,
Each quirk adds spice, it's true!

Bicycles with honking horns,
Cats in hats, oh what a sight,
Through every bump our spirit's born,
In sunny days or starry night.

Come share a pie of silly dreams,
With whipped cream swirling in delight,
It's laughter, after all, that beams,
And shines upon our quirky plight.

So here we wander, hand in hand,
With smiles to guide us on our way,
In a jest-filled, joyful wonderland,
We find our bliss in childlike play.

Tickled by Time

Time's a jester, what a prank,
With tricks and ticks, it never sank.
A wink from dawn, a giggle at night,
We dance our days in a whirlwind flight.

Moments slip like soap in a tub,
With every bubble, we just must scrub.
A chuckle here, a snort over there,
Life's grand stage, a comedic affair.

Every wrinkle tells a tale,
Of awkward falls and silly fails.
As clocks tick on, we play our part,
A slapstick show, a work of art.

So bring the cake, and pop the fizz,
For in this chaos, we find our whiz.
With every laugh, both near and far,
We tickle life, our guiding star.

The Humor of Being

Existence drips like ice cream cones,
We sit and giggle at our silly tones.
A squirrel steals lunch, oh what a sight,
It's funnies that keep our hearts alight.

In life's big circus, each role absurd,
We juggle dreams, all slightly blurred.
The clown's got tricks, and we've got cheer,
Our hearts are light when whimsy's near.

Questions swirl like cotton candy,
With sweet surprises—oh so dandy!
Philosophers ponder, we just titter,
As wisdom's punchline makes us glitter.

Laughter's our bridge to all we see,
In wobbly boats on a fizzy sea.
For in this folly, we learn to sing,
The humor in life is the real bling.

Smiles in the Serendipity

Stumbling on joys, like rocks in the stream,
We trip and we laugh, oh what a dream!
A misplaced joke, a wink from fate,
We gather our smiles, never too late.

Fortune's a baker with cakes on display,
Sprinkles of laughter in each easy sway.
The universe winks, throws us a jest,
In serendipity, we find our best.

A narrow escape from a ticklish twist,
We laugh at the moments we almost missed.
A serendipitous glance, a silly dance,
We frolic through chance, given the chance.

So here's to the quirks, to fate's clumsy hands,
To the smiles we share in life's goofy plans.
In the chaos of joy, we craft our delight,
Where nothing's too serious, all feels just right.

Grinning at Existence

In the mirror's gaze, a clownish grin,
Reflecting the shenanigans within.
A world of oddballs, each role we play,
With giggles and quirks, we greet the day.

Existence hops like a frog in the park,
Making us chuckle, igniting a spark.
The cosmos ticks with a comical grin,
Reminding us all of the fun we're in.

We build our castles of laughter and cheer,
With puns in our pockets, we hold them dear.
Life's a wild show, but oh what a play,
With every scripted joke, we find our way.

So let's toast to the silly, the offbeat routine,
To merriment piled high, like ice cream.
For in grinning at life, we make it worthwhile,
With laughter unending, how can we not smile?

Laughter's Gentle Echo

A tickle in the throat, oh what a sound,
It bounces off the walls, joy unbound.
In kitchens and in halls, let it be heard,
Life's quirks catch us off guard, absurd!

A slip on the sidewalk, a dog in a hat,
With giggles escaping, we're merry as that.
Inside of our chests, a chuckle takes flight,
Dancing through shadows, making things bright.

When life hands you lemons, make lemonade fun,
Add a splash of mischief, now you've just begun.
Sprinkled with laughter, oh what a treat,
Let's savor the moments, they're oh-so-sweet!

So grab a good friend and share tales of cheer,
With each little story, our joy will draw near.
For life is a game, and we're all in the play,
Unwrap every moment, come join in the fray.

The Warmth of a Chuckle

When morning light breaks, and yawns invade,
We stumble through life, in a sleepy parade.
With coffee in hand, spills on the floor,
We chuckle and grin, what's life for?

A cat in a tree, what a silly sight,
Meowing like crazy, with all of its might.
We can't help but giggle at all of its flair,
It's fantastic to watch, just breathe in the air.

In elevators packed, where silence holds tight,
One burps (accident-prone) and all feel the light.
From strangers to friends in a flash, oh so quick,
A moment connects us, like a joke, like a trick.

So cherish the laughter, it warms like the sun,
In the midst of the chaos, it helps us to run.
Each quip and each jest, a treasure to share,
With smiles as our currency, we haven't a care.

Mirth in the Mundane

Every chore seems mundane, a rinse and repeat,
But with dance in the kitchen, our rhythm feels neat.
A mop in the hand, I twirl like a queen,
With each little step, life's a whimsical scene.

The grocery store trip, oh what a display,
With carts that collide, making humor at bay.
We bump and we laugh, in the checkout line's snarl,
Who knew that a trip could be such a ball?

Monday meetings drone, with paper and pens,
Yet a doodle beneath makes us crack up like friends.
The boss tells a story, we smirk, oh so sly,
And suddenly we're all floating up to the sky.

So find joy in the small, through the tasks that we face,
Each chuckle a spark, fills the ordinary space.
Even in the simplest, life dances along,
To the glow of our laughter, we always belong.

The Jest of Reality

In the mirror each morning, a face looks askew,
With bedhead a masterpiece, who's that peeking through?

A wink and a grin, we begin the new day,
Reality's strange, but we laugh all the way.

Traffic is halted, a parade of red lights,
I'm stuck with my thoughts, oh, what a delight!
A bird makes a ruckus, it dives for some fries,
Their feathery antics bring laughter and sighs.

The world spins on tales, of chaos and cheer,
Like a duck with a hat, hilariously clear.
Our lives are a circus, a jest and a game,
Among all the absurd, we're never the same.

So gather your joy, let it light up the way,
In humor we find clarity, come what may.
Through twists and through turns, we dance in delight,
In the jest of our journey, everything feels right.

Footnotes of Folly

In a world of blunders and bliss,
We trip on our shoelaces with a smile,
Chasing loose change, we find pure gold,
Life's quite silly, but oh, so worthwhile.

With socks that don't match and hats tilted askew,
We dance in the rain like it's all a grand show,
Our quirks and quirks are the joy of the day,
Spinning wild tales as we stumble and go.

A pie in the face is a badge of delight,
We embrace all the goofs and the gaffes with cheer,
Trading wise truths for a moment of jest,
In folly's true footnotes, we revel each year.

So here's to the nonsense, the giggles, the glee,
To the marvelous mess that we call our own,
For amidst all the folly, a wisdom unique,
Is found in the laughter that sweetens our tone.

Rapture in the Ridiculous

With fruit hats and shoes made of foam,
We dance on the sidewalks, feeling at home,
Every slip, every trip, leads to a grin,
Celebrating the chaos that's hidden within.

The chicken's in charge at the corner café,
Cracking jokes while the customers play,
Sugar spills over, the milk's gone rogue,
Oh, the rapture we find in this glorious fog!

Here comes the dog in a superhero cape,
His sidekick a cat with a dubious shape,
Together they weave a most comical plot,
The show must go on; there's laughter to knot.

As the sun dips low with a chuckle and wink,
The clouds form a smile; oh, what do you think?
In the wild, wacky world that we gladly parade,
There's rapture in laughter that never will fade.

The Sunshine of Smirks

When the morning comes with a wink and a nod,
Coffee spills over, and we laugh at the odd,
A bird tries to whistle, but forgets its tune,
The sunshine of smirks lights up the room.

With mismatched pajamas and hair gone astray,
We dance through the morning like it's a ballet,
Cooking our breakfast, we drop all the eggs,
And giggle like kids on our rickety legs.

The cat gives a yawn; the dog takes a leap,
Each moment's a treasure; we hoard memories deep,
Around the table, jokes fly like a breeze,
In the warmth of our laughter, an unbroken ease.

As sunshine fades from the candy-floss sky,
We wrap our day up with a gleam in our eye,
For every sweet moment, we're richer, no doubt,
In the sunshine of smirks, there's no room for pout.

A Journey of Jests

Pack up your giggles; we're off on a quest,
With shoes that are squeaky, we'll put them to test,
With maps made of laughter and trails marked by puns,
Every step that we take is a race for the funs.

Through valleys of chuckles and mountains of play,
We share silly stories that brighten the gray,
In a world full of wonders, we squawk and we caw,
At the strangeness of life that leaves us in awe.

We'll hitch rides on hiccups and sail on our grins,
This journey of jests is where all joy begins,
Flip-flops and laughter, who knows where we'll go,
With friends at our side, there's nothing to slow.

So come join the ride; let's dash with no end,
In this journey of jests, we've all got to bend,
For in every chuckle, our spirits do soar,
Life's a whimsical road; let's explore it some more.

The Radiance of Riddles

In a town where quirks reside,
The squirrels wear shades with pride.
They dance on power lines with glee,
While singin' tunes of mystery.

A dog in a bowtie takes his stroll,
With whispers of wisdom, he plays the role.
And children giggle at his decree,
"If you can't find the bone, just let it be!"

The sun throws laughter, a bright array,
As shadows stretch and jump, they play.
Life's conundrums, a playful jest,
In riddles, we seek the ultimate quest.

So tiptoe through giggles, embrace the rhyme,
For every blunder, there's joy in time.
With winks and chuckles, let's revel and cheer,
In this silly riddle, we have nothing to fear.

Joy's Jigsaw Puzzle

In the box of life, pieces abound,
Some are upside down, spinning round.
A piece shaped like a slice of pie,
It fits thus, as we laugh and sigh.

The corner pieces seem so wise,
They always peek at sunny skies.
While the edges tell tales of travel,
And smiles erupt as we start to unravel.

Mix in some odd shapes, quite absurd,
One looks like a laughing bird.
Together they form a picture bright,
Of dancing socks and a dog in flight.

With every turn, the humor grows,
As we fit lives' quirks like they're prose.
In the puzzle of joy, we learn through play,
That silly moments are never far away.

The Sweetness of Sarcasm

With a wink and grin, we spin our tales,
Of coffee spills and epic fails.
"Oh look, another trip down the stairs!"
We chuckle at life's little snares.

There's humor in chaos, a taste so sweet,
Like ice cream melting, it can't be beat.
A spoonful of snark in a world of bland,
Reveals the laughter outside our planned.

Through clever quips and cheeky jibes,
We paint life with vibrant vibes.
"Are you on time?" we laugh, as we know,
That life's a parade, quite the show!

So let's raise a glass to the mischief we share,
With a sarcasm sprinkle in the air.
In the sweetness of jests, our spirits ignite,
For finding joy makes everything right.

Mirth and Metaphors

In gardens where laughter blooms like spring,
Words flutter around, oh what joy they bring.
A metaphor dances, dressed in delight,
While similes wink in the soft moonlight.

Life's a jester, wearing a crown,
With mishaps and giggles, a silly renown.
Each slip and slide, a poetic tale,
Where the absurdity can never fail.

A rainbow of oddities fills the air,
As metaphors twirl, none with a care.
"Dreams are like pancakes," we chuckle with ease,
"Flip them just right, they might just please!"

So gather your words, let the fun unfurl,
In the tapestry woven, laughter's our pearl.
Embrace every moment, let freedom ring,
For in Mirth and Metaphors, our hearts take wing.

Sacred Snickers

In a world of frowns, we find our spark,
A joke, a pun, igniting the dark.
With giggles shared beneath the sky,
We chase the gloom as days go by.

Flip the script, let humor reign,
In a cosmic dance, we feel no pain.
The little quirks, they steal the show,
In sacred snickers, our spirits grow.

Life's oddities, a merry jest,
Finding joy in every quest.
As laughter loops, we join the ride,
With smiles wide, no need to hide.

So raise a glass to silly things,
And all the joy that laughter brings.
For in each chuckle, we come alive,
In sacred snickers, we thrive and jive.

Joyful Contradictions

Oh, how we stumble and then we glide,
In clumsy steps, our hearts abide.
With every twist, a laugh erupts,
Through life's absurd, we're happily ups.

A serious face, then chaos breaks,
In serious times, we make mistakes.
As logic falls and nonsense sings,
In joyful contradictions, laughter springs.

The heavy burdens we choose to bear,
Lighten with giggles, buoyed in the air.
Every fumble, a reason to smile,
In joyful twists, we go the extra mile.

So let's embrace the weird and wide,
Dance in the rain, let humor glide.
In every paradox, we find our glue,
Joyful contradictions, life's wacky brew.

The Grin of the Cosmos

Stars above, they wink and nod,
In the cosmos' grin, we get awed.
Galaxies whirl in a comical scheme,
Their cosmic laughter fuels our dream.

From asteroids bouncing like silly clowns,
To planets twirling in funny gowns.
The universe chuckles, we catch its tone,
In stardust trails, we're never alone.

Through black holes and supernova shows,
Life humor shines, and wonder grows.
In cosmic jest, we play our part,
The cosmos grins, it warms our heart.

So let's throw our heads back and laugh out loud,
With friends from beyond, we're part of the crowd.
In celestial jest, we feel so free,
The universe smiles; come share its spree.

Life's Comic Relief

When life throws pies, we'll duck and dive,
In every splat, we'll learn to thrive.
With silly faces and playful cheers,
Life's comic relief, assuaging fears.

Through ups and downs, we weave our tale,
Finding humor where others pale.
In comic strips, reality bends,
With every punchline, our joy transcends.

So let's toast to blunders, big and small,
In wobbly wits, we're having a ball.
For in each giggle, the world repairs,
Life's funny moments, like freshening airs.

Embrace the jests that come our way,
In laughter's light, we find our play.
So here's to the blushes, the slips, the spree,
Life's comic relief, as sweet as can be.

Playful Perspectives

A cat in a hat sings a tune,
With shoes made of cheese, it's quite the boon.
The sun wears a smile, with shades on tight,
While clouds drift by, in a fluffy flight.

A dog on a skateboard, what a strange sight,
Chasing after rainbows with all of its might.
Each giggle a spark, each snort a delight,
Life's silly moments make everything right.

The Canvas of Joy

Brushes dipped in laughter paint the sky,
With polka dots dancing, oh my, oh my!
The trees all sway with a whimsical flair,
While flowers burst forth with a jig and a pair.

The rivers chuckle as they flow on by,
With frogs in bowties croaking sweet lullabies.
A merry parade of quirky delight,
Where whimsy and joy unite, shining bright.

Radiance in the Absurd

Nonsense reigns where the oddballs meet,
With jellybean shoes and a marshmallow seat.
The fish wear tuxedos, oh what a scene,
As they dance on the water, so smooth and serene.

A penguin with sunglasses tells jokes by the shore,
While iguanas in tuxes hold their own galore.
From hiccups to snickers, the joy never ends,
In this world of wonder where laughter transcends.

A Tapestry of Tickles

Weaving together the quirks and the grins,
Where squirrels wear ties and revel in wins.
A pancake flips high, with syrup that flows,
Creating jigs of delight, as whimsy grows.

With giggles as stitches, we patch every tear,
Dancing in circles with love in the air.
Spinning tales from the joys that we keep,
In this tapestry of tickles, we joyfully leap.

Lighthearted Musings on Mortality

Life's a silly dance, oh so frail,
We trip and stumble, giggle and wail.
With every wrong step, a smile we find,
In this circus of life, we're all intertwined.

So cheers to the quirks, the slips and the falls,
When life throws a curve, just answer the calls.
We wear our mistakes like a badge of cheer,
Embracing the chaos, we stand without fear.

Like clowns in a ring, we juggle our fate,
With laughter as fuel, we lighten the weight.
In the game of existence, we play with glee,
Finding joy in the questions of 'who' and 'me.'

So raise up your glass, let's toast to our quirks,
For in the grand play, we're the joyful jerks.
With humor our compass, we navigate strife,
Celebrating the wonder of this wacky life.

Joyful Jests and Existential Queries

What tickles the mind, what fuels the soul?
A riddle of life, a playful goal.
The deeper we ponder, the sillier it gets,
With riddles and chuckles, no room for regrets.

So why not enjoy the absurdity here?
With a grin and a wink, let's abandon the fear.
As we chase after meaning, in jest we will play,
The questions grow lighter, like clouds on a day.

From graves to giggles, the contrasts collide,
In the theater of life, we giggle and slide.
Why frown at the end when we can just grin?
With each laugh we gather, a new life begins.

So wear your best smile, let the riddles flow,
In the circus of thoughts, we'll steal the show.
Let's ponder and laugh at the great unknown,
For joy's the best answer we've ever been shown.

The Joyful Paradox

In a world full of puzzles, we skip and we hop,
While questions abound, let's clap and not stop.
The paradox blooms in the jokes that we share,
As truths and absurdities dance in the air.

With life as a riddle, it twists and it bends,
But humor, dear friends, is the means to our ends.
So let's sing our confusions, our smirks take the stage,
In this carnival of life, let's laugh to engage.

We ponder and ponder, what does it all mean?
But wrapped in our laughter, we're not so routine.
Each chuckle a puzzle, each snort a delight,
Finding joy in the chaos, we reignite.

Embrace the odd moments, let giggles take flight,
For in each little quirk, there shines out a light.
When asked about meaning, with joy we reply,
In the laughter we share, we learn how to fly.

Whispers of Delight

In the quiet of evening, a chuckle resounds,
With shadows and giggles, our spirit abounds.
A whisper of joy floats through the air,
Tickling the senses, banishing despair.

The sun sets softly, gold spills on the grey,
While playful whispers lead us astray.
In the gentle twilight, we ponder and muse,
Life's riddles are funny, we embrace the odd clues.

Every moment we chase like a game of charades,
In laughter we flourish, our troubles cascade.
With each giggle shared, a bridge we create,
To dance with existence, to celebrate fate.

So let's keep it whimsical, this journey we roam,
In the heart of the laughter, we find our true home.
The whispers of delight, oh how they resound,
In the echoes of joy, our bliss can be found.

www.ingramcontent.com/pod-product-compliance
Lightning Source LLC
Chambersburg PA
CBHW072149200426
43209CB00051B/905